21 Poems

Suad Abdi

Tellwell Talent
www.tellwell.ca

ISBN
978-0-22887-292-4 (Paperback)
978-0-22887-293-1 (eBook)

Africa Free

Free, Free, Free
Africa Free!
African lands, oceans and seas.
We need to end the old and new African colony.
Foreign governments steal from each African country.
Africa Free, Free, Free
While others mug the wealth, Africans live in poverty.
Dictators give resources away, managing the robbery.
Those who speak up are prisoned and labeled conspiracy.
Africa Free, Free, Free
Drought and famine hits, then the world send charity.
With billions stolen, giving back little help, big calamity.
No wonder many left Africa and became refugee.
Free, Free, Free
Africa Free!

An Old Man

An old man that sits all day in his chair.
He does not smile much and couldn't care.
Speaks little and the words are unclear.
Choices of words are negative meant to flare!
Not knowing what to expect from him, just like from
a bear.
Didn't anyone tell him it is rude to stare?
He knows what he is doing, he is fully aware.
Was he always like this, or is it the wear and tear?

Forever Young!

Forever young!
Age has nothing on me.
I don't watch my tongue.
What will be, will be!
Always having fun.
My clock stopped at 23.
On paper I am 41.
Living the life of the free.
If someone told me to settle down, I run!
Who wants a family?
Listen up hun!
I know you want to be me!

Gasoline

Benzene added to gasoline?
Your words are flammable and mean.
I hold back my anger; I don't want to make a scene.
How I feel about this, I must come clean.
Stop talking to me as if I am your teen.
Please leave your crown for a minute my queen.
Do you eat steak and others eat sardine?
You've over exceeded your daily caffeine.
Was a human, and now a machine!

HATE

HATE IS A HATE IS A HATE IS A HATE!
Because someone looks different or not from your faith,
Does not justify treating them with hate.
How you look and your background, did you create?
If I was you and you me, would you still hate?

It is lack of knowledge and ignorance to discriminate.
Hatred is not small, medium or large; it's all hate.
Can you be civil or you need regulators to regulate?
Is there anything you love or do you only know hate?
Rethink your thought and your doings before it's too late.

Hate crimes come only from those groups that hate.
We can't control of how long we live, but how we relate.
When you hate yourself, you can only reflect hate.
Know your words and actions will decide your fate.
HATE IS A HATE IS A HATE IS A HATE!

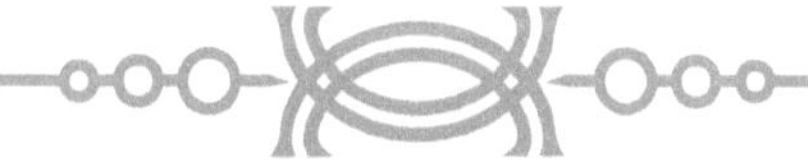

Hearing the children's laughter

Hearing the children's laughter
One after one, after one, after one
They are full of wonder
Always having fun
They race, who is faster
All of them have won
In front of my home they gather
They ring the bell, and then they run
Who do they take after?
Of course everyone!

HOPE

Optimism is hope.
In bad situation one must cope.
Tomorrow will be better, ignore your horoscope.
See the real magic from a telescope.
Be aware of a slippery slope.
Don't wait till your hanging by the rope.
We live on a small globe.
Dream big and start pushing the envelope.

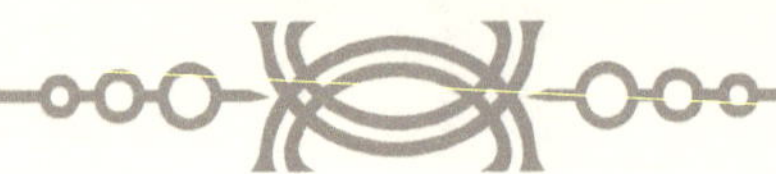

I AM NOT TOBY

Get my name right, I am not Toby!

I don't do as you say.

I don't say as you wish.

I don't jump when you tell me to.

I don't care what you think.

Get my name right.

I am not Toby!

JUST BOSS OFF

Here comes trouble.
Lives in a bubble.
Makes your work double.
Turns place into rubble.

He said there is an issue.
He added work and said, continue.
Will I need a tissue?
Totally lacking virtue.

I'm tired of this stuff.
Enough is enough!
My middle name is rough.
Just boss off.

My Canada

A land where the indigenous are respected, and
reconciliation is done as they see.
A land where the Charter of Rights and Freedoms are
practiced and people are free.

A country where there is no hate, inclusion and unity
is the key.
A country that is great with its people and economy.

My Canada is green and there is no poverty.
My Canada is the best place in the world to be.

No Perfection Nonetheless!

Pros and cons.
Right and wrong.
Yes and no.
Come and go.
Good and bad.
Happy and sad.
True and Fake.
Add and take.
Plus and minus.
Strength and weakness.
More and less.
No perfection nonetheless!

Oldcomer

I'm an oldcomer.
They still call me new.

I didn't arrive this summer.
The new are few.

Due to my head cover,
You think I'm brand-new.

Treating me like a sucker.
I've lived here longer than you.

As we speak you discover.
How little you really knew.

PANDEMIC

Is it an endemic, epidemic or pandemic?
It is a PANDEMIC!!!
Covering mouth and nose is the routine.
Social distancing must be seen.
Hands should be clean.
The sick have to quarantine.
Keep good hygiene.
Eat healthy cuisine.
Roll your sleeves for the vaccine.

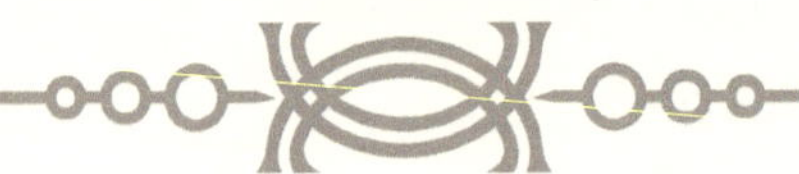

Same O Same O

The alarm gets me up.
I eat fast and drink my tea.
I'm member of the morning rush club.
Working hard, call me bee.
The best week has a pay stub.
We can all agree!

End of the day, I must go.
We said goodbye, was there a hello?
Another day that was so so!
This is five days in a row.
Nothing new, same o same o!

Something Broke

Silence!
Months go by, no talk.
Then we do.
It's a noise.
Who is wrong?
Is it you, is it me?
We don't agree.
Something broke.
You're not there.
I don't care.
Something broke.
Silence!

Stand With U

I didn't know this land's truth.
I didn't know of the residential schools.
I didn't know of the unmarked mass graves.
I didn't know the genocide by the church and the state.
I didn't know, but now that I do.
I will to stand with you.

TEA

Not too strong.
Tan to the dark side.
Sweeten just right.
After breakfast and after sun light.
Not Dr.'s orders but for my personal delight.
Surely makes my day bright.
Taking about tea, I can go on!

Telling the truth

Telling the truth.
The words will come out smooth.
The brain stays in its youth.
The soul it will soothe.
Your story can not be confused.
Lies you refuse.
Stress is reduced.
Say goodbye to the blues.
This is the life you choose.
Telling the truth.

The Sun Will Shine

Today might be cloudy, muggy and miserable
Tomorrow can become sad, blue and unbearable
You look around and everyone seems uncomfortable
But the sun will shine, and you will be just fine

Life can be cruel, mean and unfair
People might see the wrong look away and don't care
Justice can be delayed until you pull on your hair
The sun will shine and your troubles will decline

Your faith can be tested shaken and even weaken
Nothing works and you feel that you are beaten
Needing to collect yourself after being shattered and
broken
Clouds and storms come and go, but the sun will shine

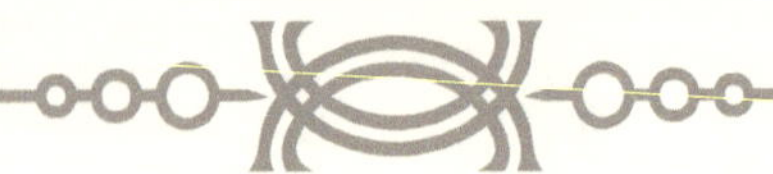

We are living a lie

We hear the nature cry.
We see the animals die.
We ask one another why.
We can't handle a hot July.
We complain about Smokey sky.
We are on a stand by.
We don't even try.
We watch time fly.
We like to deny.
We are living a lie.

Your Ways

Your ways.
Excellence you chase.

Considerate always.
Not looking to be praised.

Doing right in any case.
Fairness is your phrase.

Challenging the blaze.
Not one, but all your days.

You have the gift to amaze.
This is how you were raised.